WASTERS

RICHARD DODD

WASTERS

ISBN: 978 - 9988 - 9374 - 3 - 0

Unless otherwise stated, all scripture quotations are taken from the New International Version(NIV) of the Bible.

For any further information, contact the author on the following;

Reverend Richard Dodd
General Dodd Ministry
Adenta Baptist Church
Email: doddgeneral@gmail.com
+233(0) 245453363 / +233 (0) 546279195

Cover design: Samuel Fletcher (Fletcherrain Ideas) ~ 0246918765 // 0205813614

Contents

INTRODUCTION

In ***Hosea 4:6 KJV,*** God stated emphatically, *"My people are destroyed for lack of knowledge".*

Action in ignorance results in pain and waste of time, resources and life.

I've met people who started life with great potential and a promising future, yet with time I only realized they amounted to nothing, with some even dying before their time to depart the earth was due.

Life is not fair; it won't give you what you think you deserve but what you fight for. Yet fighting what you don't know is also a waste of time and resources.

The story is told of a widow who spent all she had to the extent of selling property to take care of her only son through to the university.

Upon completion, the widow knew her investment in her son was going to yield great fruit; believing God that her son was going to get a good job and come and take care of her. By the grace of God, the son completed his service and landed a job in an oil company, with good salary, a bungalow and a personal car. However, dear reader, that is when the waster did strike. What happened? Out of excitement, the old widow started broadcasting to family and friends what had happened, not knowing it is not everyone who hears of your achievements who is truly happy for you.

The day this young man was to report to work, on his way to the office, an articulator truck carrying a forty-footer container failed its breaks and headed straight for the vehicle this young man (the widow's son) was in. Killing everyone on board, including the young man. Everything wasted.

I have also seen people with great destinies end up no where because of what they do to themselves. Wasting destiny.

I would want you to take a journey with me as we acquire knowledge and insight as to who and what a waster is so that we will not fall victim to their activities.

CHAPTER

One

Understanding The 'Waster'

The King James Dictionary defines a *"waster"* as someone who wastes goods or consumes excessively or mindlessly.

15 *"Behold, they shall surely gather together,*
but not by me: whosoever shall gather

together against thee shall fall for thy sake. [16] Behold, I have created the smith that bloweth the coals in the fire, and that bringeth forth an instrument for his work; and I have created the waster to destroy."

~ Isaiah 54:15-16

1. *The Waster is an Army*

The waster moves like an army into your life, family or any aspect of your life and destroys anything you have laboured for, sometimes all your life.

"[2] Hear this, ye old men, and give ear, all ye inhabitants of the land. Hath this been in your days, or even in the days of your fathers? [3] Tell ye your children of it, and let your children tell their children, and their children another generation. [4] That which the palmerworm hath left hath the

locust eaten; and that which the locust hath left hath the cankerworm eaten; and that which the cankerworm hath left hath the caterpiller eaten. [5] *Awake, ye drunkards, and weep; and howl, all ye drinkers of wine, because of the new wine; for it is cut off from your mouth.* [6] *For a nation is come up upon my land, strong, and without number, whose teeth are the teeth of a lion, and he hath the cheek teeth of a great lion.* [7] *He hath laid my vine waste, and barked my fig tree: he hath made it clean bare, and cast it away; the branches thereof are made white."*

~ Joel 1:2-7 KJV

The *"waster"* arrives like an army, dispersing and smashing everything in its path. For example, everything was normal before the Russia-Ukraine conflict nevertheless, after the war started, it harmed many people and properties in both countries. The whole globe is suffering as a result of this conflict. The *"waster"* is very powerful with its operations. By the time the *"waster"* finishes what they're doing to your life, you will notice that many good things would have been wasted.

In my years of ministry, I have noticed that the *"waster"* appears after you have put in a lot of effort and labour, only to leave you suddenly with nothing. When the *"waster"* enters your life, good things are crushed.

2. *The Waster is a Devastator*

A devastator is someone who brings to a state of ruin or shock.

The *"waster"* is devastating. Allowing space for the *"waster"* is one of the worst mistakes you can ever make. You cannot allow *"wasters"* to grow and succeed in your ministry, marriage, business, education, or finances.

It is critical for you to understand as a Christian that when the *"waster"* is present in your life, you will experience numerous failures for which you will have no explanation: money will either run out or fail completely, you will begin to believe that God's work is too difficult, relationships will suffer, and everything you do will fail. Your life will be empty while the *"waster"* is there. You will get dangerously close to making a breakthrough only to be sent away.

You will have essential knowledge but fail to use it; you will have opulent property but fail to cultivate it; and you will have useful items but they will be idle. The *"waster"* will cause you to squander opportunities, spend all of your time with the wrong people, and build barriers that will prevent you from appreciating the good things in life.

God has given you talents and abilities, and the *"waster"* will cause you to waste them; your destiny, star, and gift will all perish. *"Wasters"* lead you to feel that you have no place in the world and are unworthy of anything.

Never forget that the thing that counts most in your life is the one that the *"waster"* will destroy.

For example, I recently visited someone's coconut farm, and he asked me to pray for his property due to some unexpected incidents. I wondered what the strange incidents might be. When I arrived, the coconut tree was still erect, but *"wasters"* were destroying the immature fruits. I saw something that resembled a worm and had a hard shell on its back, much like a bee. I went on to say, *"This is simply wickedness."*

I don't want you to forget that the opponent is a thief. He roars like a lion as he travels. What is his purpose? To capture, kill, or destroy. How did I become aware of this? Because ***John 10:10*** in the Bible states as much! Satan and his followers engage in more than just murder, theft, and destruction. He wastes the resources, opportunities, and advantages that God has provided for His children, according to ***Isaiah 54:16.***

He does it so often that if you are not vigilant and sober-minded enough to be aware of his schemes, he may ruin your whole future!

3. *The Waster is a Devourer*

This kind of waster comes Like A Wounded Lion.

> *"[8] Be sober, be vigilant; because your adversary the devil, as a roaring lion, walketh about, seeking whom he may devour:"* **~ 1 Peter 5:8 KJV**

Like a wounded lion, the *'wasters'* come into one's life unannounced, with force just to devour.

A devourer is one who swallows.
What this kind of waster does is to introduce fear into its victim, and then eventually swallows anything good in one's life.

What this kind of *'waster'* does is to out of their activities, drive away those who shield and cover you and then they would have the opportunity to swallow anything good and useful in your life.

4. *The Waster is a Thief*

From ***John 10:10***, you will realize that Satan is introduced as a thief who comes only to steal, kill and destroy.

The waster does not come to play. Like the devourer, they come unannounced, and then subtly,in a cunning way, steal what good thing you have in your life with the intention of destroying it.

The waster wastes:

- Life
- Time
- Families or marriages
- Money
- Destinies
- Churches or institutions
- Anything in its way.

CHAPTER Two

Weapons Of The Waster

Child of God, the waster does not come to play in the life of the believer.

The *'waster'* is well armored and equipped to do whatever the assignment and agenda is.

You will realize again from ***Isaiah 54:15-17 NIV***

"[15] If anyone does attack you, it will not be my doing; whoever attacks you will surrender to you. [16] "See, it is I who created the blacksmith who fans the coals into flame and forges a weapon fit for its work. And it is I who have created the destroyer to wreak havoc; [17] no weapon forged against you will prevail, and you will refute every tongue that accuses you. This is the heritage of the servants of the Lord, and this is their vindication from me," declares the Lord."

That the waster has well-crafted weapons. Let's look at some of them .

1. *Human beings*

While God uses human beings to be a blessing to man, the enemy is also a master of using human beings as weapons and tools to destroy.

"36 a man's enemies will be the members of his own household.'"
~ Matthew 10:36 NIV

Growing up, I saw a woman introduced in the marriage of my parents as a second wife. Believe me, she was introduced as a weapon to destroy by stealing the joy of a happy home.

I would sometimes be woken up at night with my mother almost dying because a woman introduced as a weapon, was on an assignment to steal, kill and destroy.

I've seen human beings allow themselves out of carnality and selfishness to be used as a weapon to waste churches, families and institutions.

Don't forget the waster can use yourself as a weapon to waste what you would have used years to build.

May you not use your own hands to throw out of your boat what you have gathered over time.

2. *Words*

Believe me, words are weapons.

Your words may not be the cause of all your problems, but they can cause a lot of them.

What we say or others say to us have the ability to change our world and either make it better or destroy it.

"[3] By faith we understand that the worlds were framed by the word of God, so that the things which are seen were not made of things which are visible."
~ Hebrews 11:3 (NKJV)

"Words can be like X-rays if you use them properly -- they'll go through anything.

AND SO ***Proverbs 18:21 (KJV)*** says:
"[21] Death and life are in the power of the tongue: and they that love it shall eat the fruit thereof."

Sticks and stones may break your bones, but words can change your brain.

Child of God, let's be careful of what we say and how we say it. The *'waster'*, knowing he can't do what he wants to do, will drive you to destroy your own world with what you say.

Words

- *Contain spiritual power and can be either demonic or godly.*
- *Creates an atmosphere either negative or positive*
- *Construct or destroy our destiny*

So speak & say what you want to see not what you see…

The battle of David & Goliath was a battle of words:

*"41 Meanwhile, the Philistine, with his
shield bearer in front of him, kept coming
closer to David. 42 He looked David over
and saw that he was only a boy, ruddy and
handsome, and he despised him. 43 He said
to David, "Am I a dog, that you come at
me with sticks?" And the Philistine cursed
David by his gods. 44 "Come here," he said,
"and I'll give your flesh to the birds of the
air and the beasts of the field!" 45 David
said to the Philistine, "You come against
me with sword and spear and javelin, but
I come against you in the name of the Lord
Almighty, the God of the armies of Israel,
whom you have defied. 46 This day the Lord
will hand you over to me, and I'll strike you
down and cut off your head. Today I will*

give the carcasses of the Philistine army to the birds of the air and the beasts of the earth, and the whole world will know that there is a God in Israel. [47] All those gathered here will know that it is not by sword or spear that the Lord saves; for the battle is the Lord's, and he will give all of you into our hands." **~ 1 Sam 17:41-47**

God respects what we say on earth:

"[26] The Lord said to Moses and Aaron: [27] "How long will this wicked community grumble against me? I have heard the complaints of these grumbling Israelites. [28] So tell them, 'As surely as I live, declares the Lord, I will do to you the very things I heard you say: [29] In this desert your bodies will fall — every one of you twenty years old or more who was counted in the census

and who has grumbled against me. [30] *Not*
one of you will enter the land I swore with
uplifted hand to make your home, except
Caleb son of Jephunneh and Joshua son of
Nun. [31] *As for your children that you said*
would be taken as plunder, I will bring
them in to enjoy the land you have rejected.
[32] *But you — your bodies will fall in this*
desert." ~ **Num 14:26-32**

So what the *'waster'* does sometimes is to push or manipulate men and women with great destinies to speak negatively into their own lives thereby wasting their own lives.

3. *Fear*

Fear is a weapon the 'waster' uses.

"[7] For God hath not given us the spirit of fear; but of power, and of love, and of a sound mind." ~ 2 Timothy 1:7 (KJV)

"[15] For ye have not received the spirit of bondage again to fear; but ye have received the Spirit of adoption, whereby we cry, Abba, Father." ~ **Romans 8:15 (KJV)**

After all the achievements of the prophet Elijah, one woman made him resign before his time. One statement and threat from Jezebel made this great prophet run away from town out fear. Child of God, fear is a spirit, power, an emotion or an action that the 'waster' can use as a weapon.

Fear can be described as:

- *Healthy Fear:*

This is the fear of God... Reverence, Respect or Honor towards God which shows in what we do.

"28 Wherefore we receiving a kingdom which cannot be moved, let us have grace, whereby we may serve God acceptably with reverence and godly fear:"
~ Hebrews 12:28 (KJV)

"7 By faith Noah, being warned of God of things not seen as yet, moved with fear, prepared an ark to the saving of his house; by the which he condemned the world, and became heir of the righteousness which is by faith." ***~ Hebrews 11:7 (KJV)***

"[17] Honour all men. Love the brotherhood. Fear God. Honour the king." **~ 1 Peter 2:17 (KJV)**

"[7] The fear of the Lord is the beginning of knowledge: but fools despise wisdom and instruction." **~ Proverbs 1:7 (KJV)**

This is healthy fear because it is positive and needed by any child of God. Believe me, the *'waster'* will fight the child of God from developing or walking in this kind of fear in life.

- *Natural Fear:*

This kind of fear is a *hormone* released in the body which causes, fight, flight or freeze. The stress *hormone,* cortisol, is public *health* enemy number one.

Scientists have known for years that elevated cortisol levels interfere with *learning* and *memory,* lower immune function and bone density, increase weight gain, blood pressure, cholesterol, heart disease... The list goes on and on.

Chronic stress and elevated cortisol levels also increase risk for depression, mental illness, and lower life expectancy.

This week, two separate studies were published in Science linking elevated cortisol levels as a potential trigger for mental illness and decreased resilience — especially in adolescence.

Cortisol is released in response to *fear* or stress by the adrenal glands as part of the fight-or-flight mechanism.

- *Abnormal Fear:*

This is what we call the spirit of fear or demonic fear.

This one is the weapon the *'waster'* uses.

i. This one jumps on you and fight your faith…

ii.

"30 But when he saw the wind boisterous, he was afraid; and beginning to sink, he cried, saying, Lord, save me."

~ Matthew 14:30 (KJV)

iii. It opens the door for the devil to step in; we say fear connects us to the devil while faith connects us to God…

" [10] And he said, I heard thy voice in the garden, and I was afraid, because I was naked; and I hid myself."
~ Genesis 3:10 (KJV)

iv. It makes you incompetence, unproductive, unfruitful, immobilize you, brings you to a halt and sometimes to the extreme useless and can even make you die before your time…

"And I was afraid, and went and hid thy talent in the earth: lo, there thou hast that is thine." ***~ Matthew 25:25 (KJV)***

What are the triggers of fear which is used as a weapon?

- *Some of the things we see*
- *Some of the things we hear*
- *Some negative experiences*
- *Some negative expectations*
- *Ignorance*

The devil would like to attack you through fear in these 5 areas:

1. *Fear of change.*
2. *Fear of people.*
3. *Fear of the unknown.*
4. *Fear of responsibilities.*
5. *Fear of failure.*

"[18] There is no fear in love; but perfect love casteth out fear: because fear hath torment.

He that feareth is not made perfect in love."
~ 1 John 4:18 (KJV)

"[25] For the thing which I greatly feared is come upon me, and that which I was afraid of is come unto me." **~ Job 3:25 (KJV)**

"[25] The fear of man bringeth a snare: but whoso putteth his trust in the Lord shall be safe." **~ Proverbs 29:25 (KJV)**

*"[25] And they returned from searching
of the land after forty days. [26] And they
went and came to Moses, and to Aaron,
and to all the congregation of the children
of Israel, unto the wilderness of Paran,
to Kadesh; and brought back word unto
them, and unto all the congregation, and
shewed them the fruit of the land. [27] And
they told him, and said, We came unto the*

land whither thou sentest us, and surely
it floweth with milk and honey; and this is
the fruit of it. 28 *Nevertheless the people be*
strong that dwell in the land, and the cities
are walled, and very great: and moreover
we saw the children of Anak there. 29 *The*
Amalekites dwell in the land of the south:
and the Hittites, and the Jebusites, and the
Amorites, dwell in the mountains: and the
Canaanites dwell by the sea, and by the
coast of Jordan. 30 *And Caleb stilled the*
people before Moses, and said, Let us go up
at once, and possess it; for we are well able
to overcome it. 31 *But the men that went*
up with him said, We be not able to go up
against the people; for they are stronger
than we. 32 *And they brought up an evil*
report of the land which they had searched
unto the children of Israel, saying, The land,
through which we have gone to search it, is

a land that eateth up the inhabitants thereof; and all the people that we saw in it are men of a great stature. [33] *And there we saw the giants, the sons of Anak, which come of the giants: and we were in our own sight as grasshoppers, and so we were in their sight."* **~ Numbers 13:25-33 (KJV)**

Fear is the devil's trusted weapon... You will be rewarded by the fears you conquer.

4. ***Time / Procrastination / Excuses***

You can always give yourself a reason why something can't be done.

Sometimes the reasons are excuses we give ourselves just to waste time.

I grew up hearing the proverb, *"procrastination is a thief of time"* and it hasn't changed.

"[12] Teach us to number our days, that we may gain a heart of wisdom."
~ Psalm 90:12 (NIV)

Time can be considered in three ways.

i. First, time is a trust.

As a trust, you are either:

- Frittering it away, i.e To reduce or squander it little by little
- Let it slip through your fingers,
- Squander it in wanton waste?

Or

- You treasure it,
- Use it to maximum advantage,
- Fill every minute with 60 seconds' worth of service to God?

ii. Second, time is a test.

- That is why we say someone or something stands the test of time.

Time past is time that we have no power over, but time to come lays upon each one of us the possibility of moral and spiritual choices.

Time in itself is neither good nor bad except as we make it so. But it becomes a crucial test, sifting us through and through, minute by minute.

How are you reacting to that test? How does it affect you?

iii. Third, time is an appointment.

Time has been given to us for the purpose of glorifying God in this life.

Time has been given to us to have an encounter with the living God.

However famous a person may be or however great his wealth or whatever his contribution to literature or science, if he has not come into a vital conversion experience with Jesus Christ, then that person has lived in vain.

"27 And as it is appointed unto men once to die, but after this the judgment:"
~ Hebrews 9:27 (KJV)

NOW...

"Walk in wisdom toward them that are without, redeeming the time."
~ Colossians 4:5, KJV

"[5] Behave yourselves wisely [living prudently and with discretion] in your relations with those of the outside world (the non-Christians), making the very most of the time and seizing (buying up) the opportunity." **~ Colossians 4:5, (AMPC)**

"[5] Conduct yourself with wisdom in your interactions with outsiders (non-believers), make the most of each opportunity [treating it as something precious]."
~ Colossians 4:5, (AMP)

To redeem something means to buy it back, to regain possession of it.

This is because someone said time is like a thief it can steal strength from our muscles and youth from our faces, it can rob us of our health and strip us of everything that we have.

When God says we should be *"redeeming the time,"* He wants us to live in constant awareness of that ticking clock and make the most of the time we have.

In fact, the NIV's translation of ***Ephesians 5:16*** uses the phrase making the most of every opportunity instead of redeeming the time

- It is wisdom to redeem the time because of the days we live in…

"15 See then that ye walk circumspectly, not as fools, but as wise, 16 Redeeming the time, because the days are evil."

~ *Ephesians 5:15-16 (KJV)*

Precious one, time can be used as a weapon of the *'waster'*, be wise to redeem it.

5. *Anger and offenses*

The word offence in the Bible is the word scandalon in which you get a scandal, a juicy scandal. Have you noticed how juicy scandals are?

Scandal is when someone seems to have done something wrong and the newspapers get a hold of it and they start to spread it out. Have you noticed everyone wants to talk about it and spread the scandal?

When the Bible is talking about an offence it is talking about setting a trap deliberately that would cause someone to stumble in their walk. I'll say it again. When the Bible is talking about a Biblical offence, it means setting a trap or a snare so that someone coming along trips up and falls and their journey is hindered.

Now just have a think about that. Do we make mistakes? Yes, we make mistakes. Do we sin and fail? Yes, we sin and fail. These are not offences necessarily. How we respond is the offence.

A Biblical offence is where I actually set out to do something that will trip up someone else and I'll show you how this happens.

You'll be quite surprised when you look at it, so a Biblical offence is when something is set out that deliberately stumbles or I can choose to be stumbled.

One thing that offends people, Christians particularly and also unbelievers, is the truth. The truth. Truth can deeply offend people, especially if the truth comes in the form of feedback or correction.

Now let me ask you this question. How is it possible for you to be a disciple or follower of Jesus without correction? It's impossible and don't think it all comes from Jesus.

We actually need others to talk into our life to help us see what we can't see. Don't just be so spiritual you think the Holy Ghost is going to tell you everything. We live in community, we live in relationships and when you're in relationships people get affected by our behaviour and they talk with us hopefully about what we're doing that actually is creating blocks in the relationship.

The older brother in the story of the Prodigal Son. The Prodigal Son, the Prodigal Son goes out and totally blows it, blows all the money, has a wild life, comes back in, and the father says I want to show you how grace is.

It's this big! And he forgives him and clothes him and welcomes him, has a party, and the older brother was offended. Why was he offended? You don't deserve this. The grace of God can be offensive because - this is what the older brother is thinking - I have worked so hard. Why should you get it easy? He was offended. He was offended by grace, offended by goodness.

Unmet expectations, the truth, correction or just disappointments in life, people letting us down or failing in some way all have the potential to stumble us, whether the person did it deliberately or not.

Every time someone does not meet expectations, hurts, offends, betrays, lets you down, at that point you have a decision to make - prison or promotion.

Either be imprisoned with the offence by judging or holding it in my heart, or I can be promoted by God if I will release grace into it. I can operate in faith and do it God's way. I can operate in unbelief and do what I feel to do.

When something happens you can either reach out in love and show grace, or you can react and become offended. Once you become offended - now here's where the scandal comes - it's actually sitting in your heart and once you're offended a lot of things are going to happen.

6. ***Worry / anxiety / discouragement.***

7. ***Diseases and death.***

CHAPTER

Three

Examples From Scripture

The *'waster'* does not go after just anyone. The *'waster'* looks out for those with great potentials and destinies and strategizes some times over a long period before going after them.

Two classic examples from the scriptures.

1. John The Baptist

Great potential, great achievements. But didn't end well.

"[14] King Herod heard about this, for Jesus' name had become well known. Some were saying, "John the Baptist has been raised from the dead, and that is why miraculous powers are at work in him." [15] Others said, "He is Elijah." And still others claimed, "He is a prophet, like one of the prophets of long ago." [16] But when Herod heard this, he said, "John, whom I beheaded, has been raised from the dead!" [17] For Herod himself had given orders to have John arrested, and he had him bound and put in prison. He did this because of Herodias, his brother

Philip's wife, whom he had married. 18 For John had been saying to Herod, "It is not lawful for you to have your brother's wife." 19 So Herodias nursed a grudge against John and wanted to kill him. But she was not able to, 20 because Herod feared John and protected him, knowing him to be a righteous and holy man. When Herod heard John, he was greatly puzzled; yet he liked to listen to him. 21 Finally the opportune time came. On his birthday Herod gave a banquet for his high officials and military commanders and the leading men of Galilee. 22 When the daughter of[c] Herodias came in and danced, she pleased Herod and his dinner guests. The king said to the girl, "Ask me for anything you want, and I'll give it to you." 23 And he promised her with an oath, "Whatever you ask I will give you, up to half my kingdom."

24 She went out and said to her mother,
"What shall I ask for?" "The head of John
the Baptist," she answered. 25 At once the
girl hurried in to the king with the request:
"I want you to give me right now the head
of John the Baptist on a platter." The king
was greatly distressed, but because of his
oaths and his dinner guests, he did not want
to refuse her. 27 So he immediately sent an
executioner with orders to bring John's
head. The man went, beheaded John in the
prison, 28 and brought back his head on a
platter. He presented it to the girl, and she
gave it to her mother. 29 On hearing of this,
John's disciples came and took his body and
laid it in a tomb." **~ Mark 6:14-29 NIV**

Child of God, by all standards, John the Baptist walked in great potential.

- His birth was prophesied.
- He came in the spirit of Elijah to fulfill bible prophecy.
- He was given the opportunity from heaven to identify and baptize the Messiah, Jesus Christ.
- He saw the Holy Spirit descend from the heavens and rest on Jesus as a dove.
- Jesus Himself said he, John the Baptist was the greatest.

What a destiny. Yet his end wasn't right. He was beheaded. What was it? The *'waster'*. Somewhere along the line, the *'waster'* succeeded in introducing offence.

I pray for you dear reader that in no way will the waster succeed in using any weapon to make you end in a bad way.

You will fulfill destiny and end well.

There are great destinies with great impact to make on earth with great stories to tell which don't end well.

I've seen so many of them in my short walk on earth. Either their life is cut short, they mess up or they never even walk in their set path on earth.

The last time I checked, Elijah was caught up into heaven. Elisha received a double portion of Elijahs grace and anointing. Sir, Ma, Elisha ended up performing more miracles than Elijah, can I say he had more impact, but,

i. *The mantle was not passed on.*

We are not told in scripture anyone received the mantle from Elisha like he received it from Elijah.,

" [20] Elisha died and was buried. Now Moabite raiders used to enter the country every spring. [21] Once while some Israelites were burying a man, suddenly they saw a band of raiders; so they threw the man's body into Elisha's tomb. When the body touched Elisha's bones, the man came to life and stood up on his feet."

~ 2 Kings 13:20-21 NIV

We are only t old that it is his bones which raised the dead from the scripture above.

May you start well, make an impact and pass on something great to the next generation.

ii. He died sick, while his predecessor didn't even die.;

If the one he took over from didn't die but was caught to heaven, then his story should have been better.

I see a *'waster'* at work here. It is the activity of a waster if the story doesn't end well.

2. The Israelites: The Valley of Dry Bones

From ***Ezekiel 37:1-14***, one sees dry bones and very dry bones symbolic of the Israelites, yet they were supposed to be an army.

You will realise from the story that when God asked the prophet whether the bones could live. The prophet said He God knew, meaning the true picture and state of what he the prophet saw was with and in God. For God it was an army but they were dry bones and very dry. Why?

Because of what they had been saying with their own mouths.

> *"11 Then he said to me: "Son of man, these bones are the people of Israel. They say, 'Our bones are dried up and our hope is gone; we are cut off.'"* ~ **Ezekiel 37:11 NIV**

Child of God, be careful what you say and confess, you may end up becoming it.

"[28] So tell them, 'As surely as I live, declares the Lord, I will do to you the very thing I heard you say:" ~ **Numbers 14:28 NIV**

Instead of confessing your

- *Conditions*
- *Situations*
- *Present state*
- *Present circumstances,*

Look for light concerning what is happening and speak it. Search for what is the thought and mind of God concerning what is happening to you and speak it.

May you not allow, out of ignorance, the 'waster' to waste you like the Israelites in the valley of dry bones.

CHAPTER *Four*

Dealing With The 'Waster'

1. Go For Light.

It takes a child of God who has light not to be a 'waster' and be wasted.

Light is God's recommended solution for life.

What do I mean by light?

- Light Is Truth
- Light Is Exposure
- Light Is Wisdom
- Light Is Revelation
- Light is the opposite of ignorance – one synonym of ignorance is blindness.
- Light Is Enlightenment – *to give someone greater knowledge and understanding about someone or something or a situation… (synonyms- make aware, inform, open someone's eyes, bring up to date, etc.)*

"1 In the beginning was the Word, and the Word was with God, and the Word was God. 2 The same was in the beginning with

God. [3] All things were made by him; and without him was not any thing made that was made. [4] In him was life; and the life was the light of men. 5 And the light shineth in darkness; and the darkness comprehended it not." **~ *John 1:1-5 KJV***

WHY LIGHT?

i. Light silences the *'waster'*.

ii. Light is an armour; It draws the line, creates and builds protection.

iii. The light you have access to determines the quality of your life. Light builds confidence.

iv. Light initiates greatness and sets up success.

v. Light helps to locate answers to questions and solutions to problems.

vi. Light solves hard sentences and shuts down challenges.

2. Be A Generational Thinker.

Generational thinkers

- Are selfless
- Are ready and willing to pay the price so others after them will not have to suffer.
- Build wealth and go after the blessing and not riches.
- Have a voice
- Build a name
- Have remembrance…

They are not *'wasters'* and can't and won't tolerate *'wasters'*.

Who is a Generational Thinker?

i. A generational thinker is a selfless person.

Moses in ***Exodus 32:1-35.***

ii. A generational thinker is one who is able to sow seeds for the future and generations to come.

Abraham in ***Genesis 18:16-19.***

iii. A generational thinker is not somebody who is only committed to what he wants to enjoy today but somebody who says *'If I run this race, I must make sure the next generation does not run my race, the next generation must run its own race. I must empower the next generation.'*

- But in our part of the world, it seems as if we don't pass on the baton, so one generation starts with the baton, it starts running and running and running, very hard, but somewhere in the middle, it drops the baton and keeps running without the baton because, the baton is what authorises the next person to run.

"So you get to the next person but you didn't pass on the baton, so the next person starts his race but in order to run his race, he has to go back and pick the baton that was dropped and then start half-way of the previous generation's race in order to run his own race.

"By the time he gets to start his race, the people he was in the race with have gone way ahead of him. He also runs somewhere, and drops the baton, so the next generation has to come back…

"By the time he starts to run his own race, everybody who started with him has completed, the stadium is empty but he is still running. That is our tragedy as Africa. That is why a person grows to be about forty years before he buys his first car.

"A person lives to be about 65 years before he builds his first house, sometimes 70 years before he lives in his own house., By the time he is ready to live in his own house, life has battered him so much he moves into his own house and dies. Why? Because he has been running a race that is not for him."

Lets look at some quotes from some great men which throws light on being a generational thinker.

Warren Buffett: *"SOMEONE is sitting in the shade today because someone planted a tree a long time ago."*

Mike Murdock once said that, *"A person is remembered for two things: problems they have caused and problems they have solved."* Are you causing problems or are you solving them for the future generations. More often than not, if you are not solving problems, you are actually causing them.

Jim Rohn said *"All good men and women must take responsibility to create legacies that will take the next generation to a level we could only imagine"*.

Our children's future is our responsibility.

"22 A good person leaves an inheritance for their children's children, but a sinner's wealth is stored up for the righteous."
~ Proverbs 13:22

U.S.A president Donald Trump says: he is a billionaire as a result of the foundation his grandfather Friedrich Trump built which his father Fred Trump inherited to influence his life with. A lot has been written about the Trump family.

A writer named Glenda Blair spent 12 years on her thorough history, The Trumps: Three Generations That Built an Empire.

But what was the secret behind Trump's success? Generational thinking!

Someone envisioned it and encouraged the whole family to do it.

"6 After Joshua had dismissed the Israelites,
they went to take possession of the land,
each to their own inheritance. 7 The people
served the LORD throughout the lifetime of
Joshua and of the elders who outlived him
and who had seen all the great things the
LORD had done for Israel. 8 Joshua son
of Nun, the servant of the LORD, died at
the age of a hundred and ten. 9 And they
buried him in the land of his inheritance,
at Timnath Heres in the hill country of
Ephraim, north of Mount Gaash.
10 After that whole generation had been

gathered to their ancestors, another generation grew up who knew neither the LORD nor what he had done for Israel. [11] Then the Israelites did evil in the eyes of the LORD and served the Baals. [12] They forsook the LORD, the God of their ancestors, who had brought them out of Egypt. They followed and worshiped various gods of the peoples around them. They aroused the LORD's anger [13] because they forsook him and served Baal and the Ashtoreths. [14] In his anger against Israel the LORD gave them into the hands of raiders who plundered them. He sold them into the hands of their enemies all around, whom they were no longer able to resist. [15] Whenever Israel went out to fight, the hand of the LORD was against them to defeat them, just as he had sworn to them. They were in great distress." **~ Judges 2:6-15**

3. Build Spiritual Intelligence

God created us to think 3 dimensionally…

According to our E.Q, I.Q, and S.Q… Unfortunately we use and develop the first two leaving the last which is more important…

It is more important because life is spiritual and to live and live well depends on your spirituality…

Both E.Q. and I.Q. no matter what, is limited but your S.Q. is unlimited because it depends on The Holy Spirit…

What is Spiritual Intelligence?

To be *SPIRITUALY INTELIGENT* is to;

1. To know you have the mind of Christ and use it in your daily life...

"[16] For who hath known the mind of the Lord, that he may instruct him? but we have the mind of Christ."

~ 1 Corinthians 2:16 KJV

"[15] Wherefore I also, after I heard of your faith in the Lord Jesus, and love unto all the saints, [16] Cease not to give thanks for you, making mention of you in my prayers; [17] That the God of our Lord Jesus Christ, the Father of glory, may give unto you the spirit of wisdom and revelation in the knowledge of him: [18] The eyes of your understanding being enlightened; that ye may know what is the hope of his calling, and what the riches of the glory of his

inheritance in the saints, [19] And what is the exceeding greatness of his power to us-ward who believe, according to the working of his mighty power," **~ Ephesians 1:15-19 KJV**

"And be renewed in the spirit of your mind;" **~ Ephesians 4:23 KJV**

2. To be led and driven by the Spirit…

"[16] This I say then, Walk in the Spirit, and ye shall not fulfil the lust of the flesh. [17] For the flesh lusteth against the Spirit, and the Spirit against the flesh: and these are contrary the one to the other: so that ye cannot do the things that ye would. [18] But if ye be led of the Spirit, ye are not under the law." **~ Galatians 5:16-18 KJV**

"[14] For as many as are led by the Spirit of God, they are the sons of God."

~ Romans 8:14 KJV

"Then was Jesus led up of the Spirit into the wilderness to be tempted of the devil."

~ Matthew 4:1 KJV

3. **To depend on and follow Christ Jesus for your daily living**

4. **To have spiritual insight and understanding…**

"[45] Then opened he their understanding, that they might understand the scriptures,"

~ Luke 24:45 KJV

"[17] As for these four children, God gave them knowledge and skill in all

learning and wisdom: and Daniel had understanding in all visions and dreams."
~ Daniel 1:17 KJV

"[20] And in all matters of wisdom and understanding, that the king enquired of them, he found them ten times better than all the magicians and astrologers that were in all his realm." **~ Daniel 1:20 KJV**

Why do you need spiritual intelligence in order to deal with the 'waster'?

i. Spiritual intelligence will make you be a step ahead of the devil...

ii. Those who live a spiritually intelligent life are not taken by surprise.

iii. It will enable you to live a life of dominion... that is because it will make you shine as light, and there is no way darkness can and will overshadow light...

iv. Those who live a spiritually intelligent life know what to do and don't struggle doing it. The sons of Issachar understood the times and knew what to do.They understand times and seasons.

v. Those who live a spiritually intelligent life apply Divine wisdom in all they do.

vi. Those who live a spiritually intelligent life are not controlled and manipulated in life…

vii. Those who live a spiritually intelligent life are too much for the devil, life and the world to handle…

viii. Those who live a spiritually intelligent life are bold and confident in life…

ix. Those who live a spiritually intelligent life are prophetic in nature…

x. Those who live a spiritually intelligent life live beyond their natural senses…

What Drives Spiritual Intelligence

i. Fellowship with The Holy Spirit .

"[14] The grace of the Lord Jesus Christ, and the love of God, and the communion of the

Holy Ghost, be with you all. Amen."
~ 2 Corinthians 13:14 KJV

"[1] Now there were in the church that was at Antioch certain prophets and teachers; as Barnabas, and Simeon that was called Niger, and Lucius of Cyrene, and Manaen, which had been brought up with Herod the tetrarch, and Saul.
[2] As they ministered to the Lord, and fasted, the Holy Ghost said, Separate me Barnabas and Saul for the work whereunto I have called them."
~ Acts 13:1-2 KJV

ii. Fasting, prayer and study and meditation on the word.

"[20] And whiles I was speaking, and praying, and confessing my sin and the sin of my people Israel, and presenting my supplication before the Lord my God

for the holy mountain of my God; 21 *Yea,*
whiles I was speaking in prayer, even
the man Gabriel, whom I had seen in the
vision at the beginning, being caused to fly
swiftly, touched me about the time of the
evening oblation. 22 *And he informed me,*
and talked with me, and said, O Daniel, I
am now come forth to give thee skill and
understanding." **~ Daniel 9:20-22 KJV**

*"*11 *Then said Daniel to Melzar, whom the*
prince of the eunuchs had set over Daniel,
Hananiah, Mishael, and Azariah,
12 *Prove thy servants, I beseech thee, ten*
days; and let them give us pulse to eat, and
water to drink. 13 *Then let our countenances*
be looked upon before thee, and the
countenance of the children that eat of the
portion of the king's meat: and as thou
seest, deal with thy servants.

[14] So he consented to them in this matter,
and proved them ten days. [15] And at the end
of ten days their countenances appeared
fairer and fatter in flesh than all the children
which did eat the portion of the king's meat.
[16] Thus Melzar took away the portion of
their meat, and the wine that they should
drink; and gave them pulse. [17] As for these
four children, God gave them knowledge
and skill in all learning and wisdom: and
Daniel had understanding in all visions
and dreams. [18] Now at the end of the days
that the king had said he should bring
them in, then the prince of the eunuchs
brought them in before Nebuchadnezzar.
[19] And the king communed with them; and
among them all was found none like Daniel,
Hananiah, Mishael, and Azariah: therefore
stood they before the king. [20] And in all
matters of wisdom and understanding, that

the king enquired of them, he found them ten times better than all the magicians and astrologers that were in all his realm."
~ Daniel 1:11-20 KJV

iii. Speaking in tongues…

"[20] But ye, beloved, building up yourselves on your most holy faith, praying in the Holy Ghost," ***~Jude 20 KJV***

iv. Fellowship with other spiritually intelligent people…

"[17] As iron sharpens iron, so one person sharpens another." ***~ Proverbs 27:17 NIV***

"[20] He that walketh with wise men shall be wise: but a companion of fools shall be destroyed." ***~ Proverbs 13:20 KJV***

v. Spiritual adventures…

"[25] And every man that striveth for the mastery is temperate in all things. Now they do it to obtain a corruptible crown; but we an incorruptible."

~ 1 Corinthians 9:25 KJV

vi. Consecration…

"[16] Because it is written, Be ye holy; for I am holy." ***~ 1 Peter 1:16 KJV***

Conclusion

I remember an advice my father in the Lord gave me many years ago when I was leaving him from Agona Swedru in the Central Region of Ghana to Accra the capital city of Ghana.

I had received the call of God and was on fire for Jesus, serving him in many capacities. When I told him I had the conviction to relocate to Accra the capital city of Accra, after many days of fasting, when he was convinced to release me to come to Accra , he prayed and released me. But before I finally moved, he told me *"BECAREFUL OF WASTED YEARS IN MINISTRY"*.

Believe me, this is an advice which has stayed with me for life and has guided me in all I do.

Child of God, you can live a wasted life. Your life can be wasted.

The *'waster'* is a spirit but because it is illegal for spirits to operate on earth without a human body, the waster can use,

- Your own self
- Someone else

- Circumstances or situations

So, ***1 Peter 5:8 NIV*** says

> *"[8] Be alert and of sober mind. Your enemy the devil prowls around like a roaring lion looking for someone to devour."*

The activities of the waster will;

- Destroy
- Spoil
- Corrupt
- Ruin
- Decay/ rot
- Injure
- Devour
- Steal
- Kill and eventually

- Waste

The joy of it is that, God has given us what it takes to overcome all the activities of the waster.

"[8] Be alert and of sober mind. Your enemy the devil prowls around like a roaring lion looking for someone to devour. [9] Resist him, standing firm in the faith, because you know that the family of believers throughout the world is undergoing the same kind of sufferings." ~ **1 Peter 5:8-9 NIV**

"[19] I have given you authority to trample on snakes and scorpions and to overcome all the power of the enemy; nothing will harm you." ~ **Luke 10:19 NIV**

May you live a life of dominion.

May the *'waster'* not waste anything in your life.

Receive grace to waste the *'waster'*.

www.ingramcontent.com/pod-product-compliance
Lightning Source LLC
La Vergne TN
LVHW050330160826
845677LV00014B/3582

* 9 7 8 9 9 8 8 9 3 7 4 3 0 *